ICH HABE MEINE MAMA LIEB
I LOVE MY MOM

Shelley Admont
Illustriert von Sonal Goyal und Sumit Sakhuja

Translated from English by Nicola Künkel
Aus dem Englischen übersetzt von Nicola Künkel

Library and Archives Canada Cataloguing in Publication
I love My Mom (German English Bilingual Edition)/ Shelley Admont
ISBN: 978-1-5259-1691-5 paperback
ISBN: 978 1 5259 0859 0 hardcovor
ISBN: 978-1-77268-299-1 ebook

Please note that the German and English versions of the story have been written to be as close as possible. However, in some cases they differ in order to accommodate nuances and fluidity of each language.

KidKiddos Books

Für die, die ich am meisten liebe - S.A.

For those I love the most-S.A.

Morgen würde Mamas Geburtstag sein. Das kleine Häschen Jimmy und seine beiden älteren Brüder flüsterten in ihrem Zimmer.

Tomorrow was Mom's birthday. The little bunny Jimmy and his two older brothers were whispering in their room.

„Lasst uns nachdenken", antwortete der älteste Bruder. „Das Geschenk für Mama sollte etwas ganz besonderes sein."

"Let's think," said the oldest brother. "The present for Mom should be very special."

„Jimmy, du hast immer so gute Ideen," fügte der mittlere Bruder hinzu. „Was meinst du?"

"Jimmy, you always have good ideas," added the middle brother. "What do you think?"

„Hm…" Jimmy fing an angestrengt zu überlegen. Plötzlich rief er, „Ich kann ihr mein Lieblingsspielzeug schenken – meine Eisenbahn!" Er nahm die Eisenbahn aus der Spielzeugkiste und zeigte sie seinen Brüdern.

"Ahm…" Jimmy started thinking hard. Suddenly he exclaimed, "I can give her my favorite toy — my train!" He took the train out of the toy box and showed it to his brothers.

„Ich glaube nicht, dass Mama deine Eisenbahn haben möchte," sagte der älteste Bruder. „Uns muss etwas anderes einfallen. Es muss etwas sein, das ihr wirklich gefällt."

"I don't think Mom likes trains," said the oldest brother. "We need another idea. Something that she will really like."

„Wir können ihr ein Buch schenken," rief der mittlere Bruder fröhlich.

"We can give her a book," screamed the middle brother happily.

„Ein Buch? Das ist das richtige Geschenk für Mama," antwortete der älteste Bruder.

"A book? It's a perfect gift for Mom," replied the oldest brother.

„Ja, wir können ihr mein Lieblingsbuch schenken," sagte der mittlere Bruder und ging zum Bücherregal.

"Yes, we can give her my favorite book," said the middle brother as he approached the bookshelf.

„Aber Mama mag spannende Bücher," sagte Jimmy betrübt, „und dieses Buch ist für Kinder."

"But Mom likes mystery books," said Jimmy sadly, "and this book is for kids."

„Ich glaube, du hast recht," stimmte
der mittlere Bruder zu. „Was sollen wir tun?"

"I guess you're right," agreed his
middle brother. "What should
we do?"

The three bunny brothers were sitting and thinking quietly, until the oldest brother finally said,

"There is only one thing that I can think of. Something that we can do by ourselves, like a card."

"We can draw millions of millions of hearts and kisses," said the middle brother.

"And tell Mom how much we love her," added the oldest brother.

Die drei Häschen wurden ganz aufgeregt und fingen an, die Geburtstagskarte zu basteln.

They all became very excited and started to work.

Die drei Häschen bastelten fleißig. Sie schnitten und klebten, falteten und malten.

Three bunnies worked very hard. They cut and glued, folded and painted.

Jimmy und sein mittlerer Bruder malten Herzen und Küsschen. Als sie mit der Geburtstagskarte fertig waren, malten sie noch mehr Herzen und noch mehr Küsschen.

Jimmy and his middle brother drew hearts and kisses. When they finished, they added more hearts and even more kisses.

Dann schrieb der älteste Bruder in großen Buchstaben:

Then the oldest brother wrote in large letters:

„Herzlichen Glückwunsch zum Geburtstag, Mama! Wir haben dich soooooo lieb. Deine drei Häschen."

"Happy birthday, Mommy! We love you sooooooooo much. Your kids."

Herzlichen Glückwunsch zum Geburtstag Mama

Endlich war die Geburtstagskarte fertig. Jimmy lächelte.

Finally, the card was ready. Jimmy smiled.

„Ich bin mir sicher, dass es Mama gefallen wird," sagte er und wischte seine schmutzigen Hände an seiner Hose ab.

"I'm sure Mom will like it," he said, wiping his dirty hands on his pants.

„Jimmy, was machst du denn?" rief der älteste Bruder. „Siehst du nicht, dass Farbe und Kleber an deinen Händen sind?"

"Jimmy," screamed the oldest brother. "Don't you see your hands are covered in paint and glue?"

„Oh nein…" sagte Jimmy. „Das habe ich nicht gesehen. Entschuldigung!"

"Oh, oh…" said Jimmy. "I didn't notice. Sorry!"

„Jetzt muss Mama an ihrem Geburtstag die Wäsche waschen," sagte der älteste Bruder und schaute Jimmy streng an.

"Now Mom has to do laundry on her own birthday," added the oldest brother, looking at Jimmy strictly.

„Nein! Das werde ich nicht zulassen!", rief Jimmy. „Ich wasche meine Hose selbst." Er lief ins Badezimmer.

"No way! I won't let this happen!" exclaimed Jimmy. "I'll wash my pants myself." He headed into the bathroom.

Zusammen wuschen sie die Farbe und den Kleber aus Jimmys Hose und hingen sie zum Trocknen auf.

Together they washed all the paint and glue from Jimmy's pants and hung them to dry.

Als sie zurück in ihr Zimmer gingen, schaute Jimmy kurz ins Wohnzimmer und sah dort seine Mutter.

On the way back to their room, Jimmy gave a quick glance into living room and saw their Mom there.

„Schaut mal, Mama schläft auf dem Sofa," flüsterte Jimmy seinen Brüdern zu.

"Look, Mom is sleeping on the couch," whispered Jimmy to his brothers.

„Ich bringe ihr meine Decke," sagte der ältere Bruder und rannte zurück in sein Zimmer.

"I'll bring my blanket," said the older brother who ran back to their room.

Jimmy schaute seine schlafende Mutter an. Plötzlich wusste er, was das perfekte Geschenk für sie wäre.

Jimmy was standing and looking at his Mom sleeping. In that moment he realized what the perfect gift for their Mom should be and smiled.

„Ich habe eine Idee!" sagte Jimmy, als der älteste Bruder mit der Decke zurückkam.

"I have an idea!" said Jimmy when the oldest brother came back with the blanket.

Er flüsterte seinen Brüdern etwas zu. Dann nickten alle drei Häschen mit den Köpfen und hatten strahlende Gesichter.

He whispered something to his brothers and all three bunnies nodded their heads, smiling widely.

Leise gingen sie zum Sofa und bedeckten ihre Mutter mit der Decke.

Quietly they approached the couch and covered their Mom with the blanket.

Alle drei Häschen gaben ihr ein Küsschen und flüsterten, „Wir haben dich lieb, Mama."

Each of them kissed her gently and whispered, "We love you, Mommy." Mom opened her eyes.

„Oh, ich habe euch auch ganz doll lieb", sagte sie lächelnd und umarmte ihre Söhne.

"Oh, I love you too," she said, smiling and hugging her sons.

Am nächsten morgen wachten die drei Häschen-Brüder sehr früh auf. Sie bereiteten das Überraschungsgeschenk für ihre Mutter vor.

The next morning, the three bunny brothers woke up very early to prepare their surprise present for Mom.

Sie putzten ihre Zähne, dann machten sie ihre Betten und räumten all ihr Spielzeug ordentlich in die Spielzeugkiste.

They brushed their teeth, made their beds perfectly and checked that all the toys were in place.

Anschließend gingen sie ins Wohnzimmer. Sie wischten Staub und machten den Fußboden sauber.

After that, they headed to the living room to clean the dust and wash the floor.

Als nächstes gingen sie in die Küche.

Next, they came into the kitchen.

„Ich mache Mamas Lieblingsfrühstück. Eine Scheibe Toast mit Erdbeermarmelade," sagte der älteste Bruder. „Und du, Jimmy, kannst ihr frischen Orangensaft einschenken."

"I'll prepare Mom's favorite toasts with strawberry jam," said the oldest brother, "and you, Jimmy, can make her fresh orange juice."

„Ich hole Blumen aus dem Garten," sagte der mittlere Bruder und lief aus der Tür.

"I'll bring some flowers from the garden," said the middle brother who went out the door.

Als das Frühstück fertig war, wuschen die drei Häschen das Geschirr. Dann dekorierten sie die Küche mit Blumen und Luftballons.

When breakfast was ready, the bunnies washed all the dishes and decorated the kitchen with flowers and balloons.

Die drei fröhlichen Häschen gingen in das Zimmer ihrer Eltern. Sie brachten die Geburtstagskarte, die Blumen und das Frühstück.

The happy bunny brothers entered Mom and Dad's room holding the birthday card, the flowers and the fresh breakfast.

Die Mutter saß auf dem Bett. Sie lächelte, als ihre Söhne "Geburtstagslied" sangen, während sie das Zimmer betraten.

Mom was sitting on the bed. She smiled as she heard her sons singing "Happy Birthday," while they entered the room.

„Wir haben dich lieb, Mama," riefen sie alle zusammen.

"We love you, Mom," they screamed all together.

„Das ist mein schönster Geburtstag!" sagte die Mutter und küsste ihre Söhne.

"It's my best birthday ever!" said Mom, kissing all her sons.

„Du hast noch nicht alles gesehen," sagte Jimmy und zwinkerte seinen Brüdern zu. „Du solltest dir die Küche und das Wohnzimmer anschauen!"

"You haven't seen everything yet," said Jimmy with a wink to his brothers. "You should check the kitchen and the living room!"

www.ingramcontent.com/pod-product-compliance
Lightning Source LLC
Chambersburg PA
CBHW040903070726
47599CB00035B/2290